SADDLE UP!

Clydesdale Horses

by Rachel Grack

BLASTOFF! READERS
2

BELLWETHER MEDIA · MINNEAPOLIS, MN

Blastoff! Readers are carefully developed by literacy experts to build reading stamina and move students toward fluency by combining standards-based content with developmentally appropriate text.

Level 1 provides the most support through repetition of high-frequency words, light text, predictable sentence patterns, and strong visual support.

Level 2 offers early readers a bit more challenge through varied sentences, increased text load, and text-supportive special features.

Level 3 advances early-fluent readers toward fluency through increased text load, less reliance on photos, advancing concepts, longer sentences, and more complex special features.

★ **Blastoff! Universe**

Reading Level

Grade
K

Grades
1–3

Grade
4

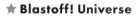

This edition first published in 2021 by Bellwether Media, Inc.

No part of this publication may be reproduced in whole or in part without written permission of the publisher. For information regarding permission, write to Bellwether Media, Inc., Attention: Permissions Department, 6012 Blue Circle Drive, Minnetonka, MN 55343.

Library of Congress Cataloging-in-Publication Data

Names: Koestler-Grack, Rachel A., 1973- author.
Title: Clydesdale horses / by Rachel Grack.
Description: Minneapolis, MN : Bellwether Media, Inc., 2021. | Series: Blastoff! readers: saddle up! | Includes bibliographical references and index. | Audience: Ages 5-8 | Audience: Grades K-1 | Summary: "Relevant images match informative text in this introduction to Clydesdale horses. Intended for students in kindergarten through third grade"– Provided by publisher.
Identifiers: LCCN 2019054255 (print) | LCCN 2019054256 (ebook) | ISBN 9781644872352 (library binding) | ISBN 9781618919939 (ebook)
Subjects: LCSH: Clydesdale horse–Juvenile literature.
Classification: LCC SF293.C65 K64 2021 (print) | LCC SF293.C65 (ebook) | DDC 636.1/5–dc23
LC record available at https://lccn.loc.gov/2019054255
LC ebook record available at https://lccn.loc.gov/2019054256

Editor: Elizabeth Neuenfeldt   Designer: Andrea Schneider

Printed in the United States of America, North Mankato, MN.

Table of Contents

Strong and Sturdy

draft horse

Clydesdales are strong **draft horses**.

One Clydesdale can pull around 7,000 pounds (3,175 kilograms)!

Clydesdales are among the largest horses. They can stand up to 18 **hands** high.

Some **stallions** weigh more than 2,000 pounds (907 kilograms)!

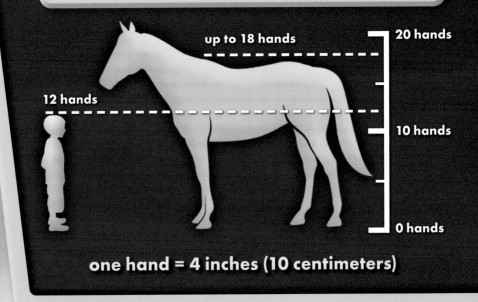

SIZE OF A CLYDESDALE HORSE

20 hands

up to 18 hands

12 hands

10 hands

0 hands

one hand = 4 inches (10 centimeters)

Most Clydesdales have **bay** or brown **coats**. Others can have black coats.

COAT COLORS

bay

brown

black

Their faces often have
white markings.

Clydesdales have **feathering** on their legs. It hangs over their big, heavy **hooves**.

Many also show **cow hocks** from behind.

cow hocks

feathering

Clydesdale Beginnings

Clydesdales were first **bred** in Scotland around 1715.

The Duke of Hamilton wanted strong horses to help farmers move heavy things.

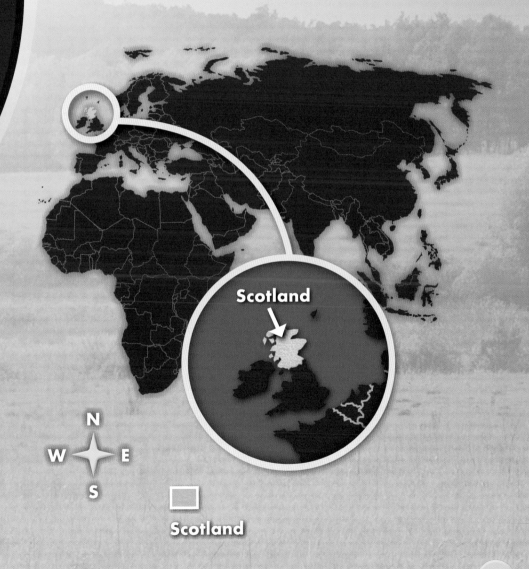

Scotland

N
W E
S

Scotland

Settlers brought Clydesdales to North America in 1842. Some people used these horses to plow fields.

Clydesdales plowing a field

CLYDESDALE HORSE TIMELINE

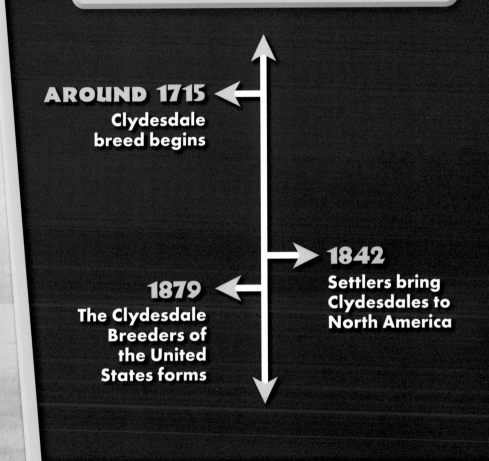

AROUND 1715
Clydesdale
breed begins

1842
Settlers bring
Clydesdales to
North America

1879
The Clydesdale
Breeders of
the United
States forms

In 1879, the Clydesdale
Breeders of the
United States formed.

Clydesdales are hard to scare. This makes them great horses for new riders.

Some Clydesdales also serve as **therapy animals**!

harnesses

Clydesdales make great
driving horses. In shows,
they wear fancy **harnesses**
and collars.

Some Clydesdales also carry heavy drums in parades!

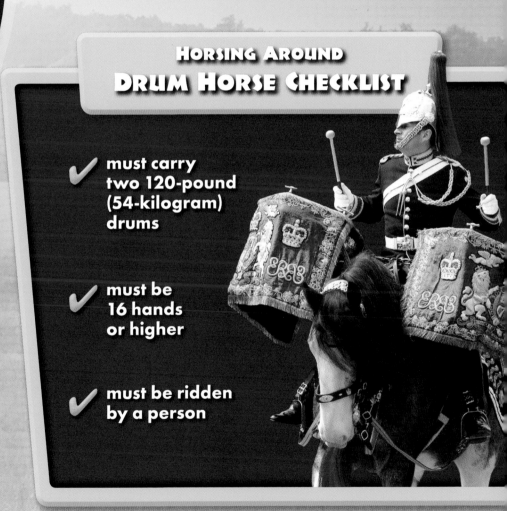

Horsing Around
Drum Horse Checklist

✓ must carry two 120-pound (54-kilogram) drums

✓ must be 16 hands or higher

✓ must be ridden by a person

Clydesdales are big, but they are light on their feet. They have a clean, high **prance**.

prance

There is more to these gentle giants than just their strength!

Glossary

bay—a coat color with a reddish-brown body and a black mane, tail, and ears

bred—mated with other horses to make horses with certain qualities

breeders—people who mate two horses to make a horse with certain qualities

coats—the hair or fur covering some animals

cow hocks—lower back legs on some animals that bend inward so they are very close together

draft horses—large, strong, and heavily built horses used for pulling heavy things

driving horses—horses that wear harnesses and pull carts, sleighs, plows, or carriages

feathering—long silky hairs on the lower legs of horses

hands—the units used to measure the height of a horse; one hand is equal to 4 inches (10 centimeters).

harnesses—sets of straps and fittings used to tie a horse to a wagon, cart, or plow

hooves—the hard coverings on the feet of animals such as horses and pigs

prance—high, springy steps

stallions—male horses

therapy animals—animals that comfort people who are sick, hurt, or have a disability

To Learn More

AT THE LIBRARY

Dell, Pamela. *Clydesdales*. New York, N.Y.: AV2 by Weigl, 2019.

Diedrich, John. *Clydesdale Horses*. North Mankato, Minn.: Capstone Press, 2018.

Meister, Cari. *Clydesdale Horses*. Mankato, Minn.: Amicus, 2019.

ON THE WEB

FACTSURFER

Factsurfer.com gives you a safe, fun way to find more information.

1. Go to www.factsurfer.com.

2. Enter "Clydesdale horses" into the search box and click 🔍.

3. Select your book cover to see a list of related content.

Index